ELIJAH AND THE BULL-GOD BAAL

Words by Norman C. Habel
Pictures by Jim Roberts

P A PURPLE PUZZLE TREE BOOK

COPYRIGHT © 1972
CONCORDIA PUBLISHING HOUSE,
ST. LOUIS, MISSOURI
CONCORDIA PUBLISHING HOUSE LTD.,
LONDON, E. C. 1
MANUFACTURED IN THE
UNITED STATES OF AMERICA
ALL RIGHTS RESERVED
ISBN 0-570-06521-6

Concordia Publishing House

When Solomon died,
the people went wild,
and everyone took sides.

Some followed one king
and some followed another.
Some followed a king down south
and some followed a king up north.
The kings down south were bad enough,
but the kings up north were worse.

They danced around a wild god,
the bellowing bull-god Baal.
They said the thunder was his roar
and the lightning was his tail.

So God sent forth His prophets,
men with long, black hair
and eyes like burning fire.
You could feel that God was angry
when they yelled His holy words.

A prophet called Elijah
was sent by God one year
when Ahab was the king up north
and jeering Jezebel his queen.

Oh, that queen was bad, lad,
very, very bad!
She liked to kiss the face of Baal
and jeer to make God mad.

Well, God was mad all right
as Elijah yelled His words
all across the land:

No rain will fall,
No dew will fall,
For many long years!

King Ahab got so angry
and jeering Jezebel so mad
that they screamed aloud to Baal,
their bellowing bull-god Baal:

Kill! Baal, kill!
Hail! Baal, hail!
Charge Elijah with your horns
and kill him with your tail!

Then Elijah came to visit Ahab
and jeering Jezebel, his queen.
"Are you the louse," King Ahab said,
"who brought this drought
on every man and every mouse
in every field and every house?"

"No!" said bold Elijah,
"the fault is all your own.
Because you worship Baal
instead of loving God,
you have brought this drought
on every man and every mouse
in every field and every house."

But jeering Jezebel just jeered
and Ahab wouldn't listen.

So Elijah said,
"Let's test your god
on top of old Mount Carmel.
You can bring your prophets,
400 men or more.
I will stand alone,
and then we'll see
whose god is God, for sure."

The people climbed up Carmel
and waited for the show.
They killed two bulls
and laid them out
on two piles of wood.
One bull was for the Baal prophets,
and one was for Elijah.

This was the test
they had arranged
to see which god was God:
The god who sent down fire
to burn up all his bull
would win the duel of the day
and show that he was God.

The Baal prophets danced and leaped
around and around their wood.
They slashed themselves
and gashed themselves;
they splashed themselves
and smashed themselves
to make their god send fire.
But nothing seemed to happen.

"Yell a little louder!"
old Elijah laughed.
"Maybe Baal is fast asleep
or thinking very hard.
Perhaps he's somewhere on a trip
or busy in the bathroom."

But the prophets kept on screeching
to their bellowing bull-god Baal:
"Fire! Baal, fire!
Hail! Baal, hail!
Send down fire from your nose
and lightning from your tail!"

When evening came,
Elijah built an altar out of stone
and placed the wood on top.
He set the pieces of the bull
over all the wood.
Three times he poured
four jugs of water over everything.

Then Elijah prayed:
"God, I know You are God
and You made everything.
Send Your fire now
and help these men repent."

CRAAAAAACK!
The sky was split in two
as fire flashed from God.
And all that was left
of the wood and meat and stones
was a few silver ashes.

The people cried aloud,
"Yahweh! Yahweh is God!"

Elijah said to Ahab,
"I can hear the sound of water
rushing down from heaven.
The drought will soon be broken,
for Yahweh, HE IS GOD!"

Elijah sat on old Mount Carmel
with his head between his knees,
and he told his servant at his side:
"Look toward the sea, my boy,
and see what you can see."

The boy came back and said:
"There's nothing there at all."
Seven times the boy looked out,
but he couldn't see a thing.
Elijah sent him one more time,
and he saw a little cloud.
It was floating like a feather
and rising like a hand
from the water of the sea.

Elijah sprang onto his feet
and called to angry Ahab:
"Get your chariot ready;
a storm is on the way
with blue-black, billowing clouds
and streams of heavy rain
to break this long, long drought."

Elijah was so excited
and full of the Spirit of God,
he ran ahead of the chariots
all the way back home
before the great rains came.

For Elijah was a bold man
in God's purple puzzle plan,
who showed the king and queen
whose God was really God.
For in the hand of Yahweh
are fire, drought, and rain.
And that's the kind of thing to know
every time they come.

OTHER TITLES